I have had a holiday, and I'd like to take it up professionally.

ALLO

PEPSI
PEPSI
PEPSI
PEPSI

Coca-Cola

8
TUNISAIR
TUNISIE TELECOM

Billabong

toni
9

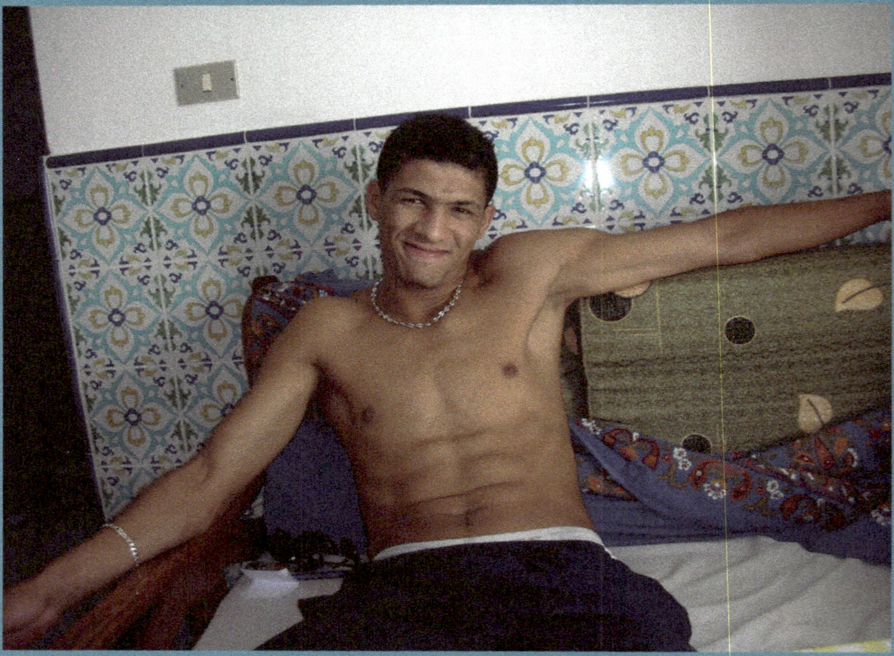

CPSIA information can be obtained
at www.ICGtesting.com
Printed in the USA
BVHW021348140319
542674BV00013B/155/P

9 780368 408779